TABLE OF CONTENTS

MW00511862

Preface

If I managed to open my mind like a flower of lotus, I would be very happy.
—Rengetsu (1791-1875) poet and nun

There are few plants on this earth that capture one's attention to immediately convey a feeling of the beauty, wonder, and mystique of nature. The lotus is one of those rare gifts; it enthralls and charms those lucky enough to behold it. This universal fascination and attraction affects us all—pond owners, poets, spiritualists, artists, gardeners, even scientists and historians.

It was our great pleasure to write this booklet for the International Waterlily & Water Gardening Society (IWGS) to show off the lotus to its audience of current admirers, plus introduce it to readers who have not yet been captivated by *Nelumbo*'s charms. We gathered information and photographs from dozens of lotus experts and enthusiasts the world over to more accurately relay how lotuses grow, as well as their great significance, which extends far beyond the water's edge. Without the help of many, this booklet would never have been written.

So whether the lotus is a beautiful flower for your pond, a source of food or medicine, a symbol for compassion and enlightenment, or an object of research, we hope this engages you further. Our goal is to provide a basic overview of how to grow and care for lotus, along with information to show the depth of its character. This short work does not have enough space to do *Nelumbo* justice; it is not a lotus compendium or a cultivar encyclopedia. Those wishing for more depth about this multifaceted plant should check the Resources section.

In closing, we hope you will learn something about the amazing *Nelumbo*, be captivated by it, and be inspired to grow or visit lotuses up close and personal. Once you do, then you will also see why this classic plant has endured through the millennia.

Aquatically Yours,
Kelly Billing and Paula Biles

Botanical Background

All Lotuses are not *Nelumbos*

Throughout mythology and history the words describing waterlilies and lotuses have been used interchangeably. This is still the case in many foreign languages, where the words "waterlily" and "lotus" can mean either *Nymphaea* or *Nelumbo*, or both. The most common aquatic confusions are the "Blue Lotus" from Ancient Egypt that refers to the blue waterlily, *Nymphaea caerulea;* the "Egyptian Lotus" that is *Nymphaea lotus,* a white night bloomer; and the subgenus of *Nymphaea* called *Lotos*. The precise use of lotus for aquatic plants designates the *Nelumbo* family, which includes two species and many hundreds of cultivars.

To make matters even more confusing there are several terrestrial plants called lotus. They include *Lotus corniculatus*, the birdsfoot trefoil; *Lotus*, a genus of the pea family; and *Ziziphus lotus*, a small tree with fruit made into wine that ancient Greeks believed to cause forgetfulness and serenity. Understandably, numerous articles have been written about the confusion of the plant name lotus. To make things perfectly clear, in this booklet lotus means *Nelumbo*.

Relationship of Lotuses to Waterlilies

There are obvious visual differences between *Nymphaea* and *Nelumbo*: the leaf shape, seed pod formation, and overall stature. But some taxonomists had previously classified lotus as a waterlily, stirring up quite a bit of controversy. Recent DNA testing has supported that *Nelumbo* be placed in its own family, separate from *Nymphaeaceae*.

The taxonomy for lotus is:

Order	*Nymphaeales*	
Family	*Nelumbonaceae*	
Genus	*Nelumbo* Adans.	
Species	*Nelumbo lutea* Willd.	
Species	*Nelumbo nucifera* Gaertn.	
Cultivar example	*Nelumbo* 'Chawan Basu'	

Species

N. nucifera

Nelumbo nucifera and *N. lutea* are the only confirmed species of lotus. The native range of *N. nucifera* is throughout Asia, Persia, India, Sri Lanka, Indonesia, Iran, Korea, Cambodia, Thailand, Vietnam, Japan, China, the Volga River delta, and Northern Australia. Comparatively, the distribution range for *N. lutea* is southeastern Canada, East and Central United States, south into Mexico, the Caribbean, and northern South America.

N. lutea

The lotus is an ancient plant, sometimes referred to as a living fossil. Because it has been around for so long and grows in so many places around the globe, even the species have countless common names. *N. nucifera* has been referred to as Sacred Lotus, Hindu Lotus, Asian Lotus, East Indian lotus, or Chinese lotus. *N. lutea* has been called lotus lily, pondnut, winkapin, water chinquapin, duck acorn, yellow lotus, and American Lotus.

Cultivars

Although there are only two existing *Nelumbo* species, several hundred cultivars are grown around the world, perhaps as many as a thousand. The lotus has been cultivated internationally for thousands of years for food, beauty, and other uses. As

a result many cultivars have come and gone, even though dozens of new ones are being created regularly.

In recent decades there has been renewed interest in new cultivars. Among other things, hybridizers in many countries strive for long term stability, vigor, pest and disease resistance, flowering capacity, and tuber production. Once suitable plants have been developed, they formally name their new plants. Of those, only a select few display all the necessary qualities to make it to market. Unfortunately common names are not consistent in the trade within each country, nor is the accurate use of cultivar names. Sometimes this is caused because hybrids may be developed by hobbyists and not produced in quantity for the trade. In addition, the hundreds of common and trade names used in different countries were never recognized or officially listed on an international level. This is often because many are hybridized in Asia and the transliteration to English names and/or meaning is confusing at best. As the world marketplace becomes better connected and technology advances, work progresses to get consistent and accurate international lists of all *Nelumbo* cultivars. (As the international *Nelumbo* registration authority, the IWGS is working on this.)

Types of Lotuses

Lotuses can be categorized in several ways: by blossom color and shape, by plant size, or by plant hardiness. As has already been mentioned, there are many hundreds of *Nelumbo* cultivars — too many to list. The photographs throughout this booklet will provide an idea of the tremendous variety in range of colors, forms, and sizes.

Plant Sizes—Bowl, Dwarf, Medium, and Large

Lotus cultivars are available in a range of sizes to fit virtually any growing area, from a small teacup to a large lake.

Individual performance depends upon climate and cultivation. However in general, characteristics of each type are listed below.

Bowl lotuses are Chinese cultivars bred to grow in the smallest containers. They can be grown in a pot under 11" (28 cm) diameter; their flower diameter is approx. 4–5" (10–13 cm); and leaves stand approximately 13" (33 cm) in height with an average diameter of 9–12" (23–30 cm).

Dwarf lotuses are slightly larger than bowl cultivars. Their leaves mature to about 1–2' (30–61 cm) high and the plants are best suited to containers 16–20" (41–51 cm) in diameter.

Medium cultivars reach 2–4' (61–122 cm) tall and grow best in a container 18–30" (46–76 cm) in diameter.

Large cultivars range from 4–8' (122–244 cm) in height. They prefer to have more freedom in their growing containers, 24–48" (61–122 cm) diameter. They also thrive in lotus bogs (mini-ponds created just for the lotus) and love to run wild in natural bottom ponds.

Plant Hardiness—Hardy and Tropical

Hardy lotuses begin their growth from rhizomes during late spring to early summer, depending upon severity of the winter and climate. Their peak flowering times are mid to late summer, dependent upon cultivar, annual weather patterns, and climate zone. Hardies go dormant by late fall and will only bloom during the summer, although some cultivars persist into fall. They are sparse bloomers compared to tropical lotuses, with larger tubers. Larger hardy lotuses have 2–3" (5–8 cm) diameter tubers.

Garet Uemura lives in Hawaii and grows the less common **tropical** lotus as well as hardies. He provided this information, gathered from his and Betsy Sakata's first-hand observations for tropical lotus in their climate. All of Garet's were collected in Thailand, India, Cambodia, and Indonesia. There was one from Japan, but it originally came from SE Asia. When he explored SE Asia, he found that the lotus in Vietnam tend to be hardy

Tropical lotus with rhizomes

lotus rather than tropical. Tropical lotuses grow in humid tropical and subtropical climates where there are no killing frosts and pond waters never freeze.

Tropicals do not exhibit the deciduous traits of hardies and most cultivars will bloom all autumn and into winter since they do not go entirely dormant, although the growth does slow down. Tropical lotuses are prolific bloomers, producing 3–4 times as many flowers as hardies. The rhizomes are thin compared to hardy lotus, from pencil diameter to about 1–1.5" (3–4 cm) in diameter. The lobes in leaves

seem to be more pronounced in certain cultivars. The flowers are double or single—pink, light pink, or white with no yellows or changeable. There are some smaller growing cultivars but there are no true miniatures as with the hardy bowl lotus.

Unless otherwise noted in this booklet, all lotus references will be to hardy cultivars and both species, which are also hardy.

Plant Structure

The lotus grows from a submerged, segmented root system. It is composed of a branching system of horizontal stems which often spread rapidly during the growing season. In their initial stage they are called runners. Late in the season they thicken to become rhizomes or tubers. The actual roots are very short growths that come out from the nodes (joints) between segments. Leaves and flowers grow from the nodes, each one on a separate prickly stem.

Buds form and last a long time before becoming blossoms with exposed central receptacles for the reproductive parts of the flower. The color, number, shape,

Flower

Leaf

and size of the petals and flowers vary greatly, as can be seen in the photographs on page 7. Color forms may be white, red, pink, multicolor, or yellow. Whether hardy or tropical, small or large, lotuses are classified by the number of petals the flower has. They are categorized as single (25 or fewer petals), semi-double (25–50 petals), or double (50 or more).

Water will bubble showing release of O_2.

Both species, *N. nucifera* and *N. lutea*, have single flowers. It is the many cultivars that comprise the complete range of flower types. Some cultivars are even double-headed or change petal color on successive days. The flower's fragrance depends upon the cultivar.

Nelumbo are perfectly designed to harness sunlight for photosynthesis, transferring gases back and forth from the atmosphere into the submerged anaerobic soil. Most parts of the plant are composed of numerous channels that function as air transport pipes. It is thought that some are for exclusive use of oxygen and others solely for carbon dioxide. Cross sections of rhizomes and stems (flower or leaf) clearly show the pipe structure. On sunny days a drop of water placed on a leaf will bubble where it joins the stem, as unused oxygen is released.

Life Cycle

The best time to carefully divide lotus and to plant tubers is after all danger of freezing is gone, while the tubers are completely dormant. Once new growth forms it becomes more difficult to extract the tubers without breaking the growing tips. New growth from the dormant tuber typically appears in late spring. Shoots come up from the joints in the rhizome and become small floating leaves. With increases in temperature, new underground runners grow and additional leaves form, this time rising above the surface. The leaves emerge tightly rolled up, then gradually unfurl. The appearance of aerial leaves indicates the time

to fertilize, since much of the energy stored in the thickened rhizomes has been used.

As the season progresses, sunlight increases in strength and daily duration, the crucial factor to make water temperatures rise. The lotus continues to create a mass of branching runners, with small short roots at each joint. The nodes are also where prickly petioles form to become leaves. Then after about two to three months of sustained 75–85°F (24–29°C) temperatures, the joints also produce stems for flowers.

During the peak blooming season every node produces a bud. It may be up to 20 days before the bud emerges as a flower. All lotuses are day bloomers, with flowers lasting 3 to 4 days. The specific times vary by climate zone, local conditions, and cultivar. In general, the first day flower opens and closes in the early morning. On the second day it opens a little later and is most active for pollination. The third day it opens with the largest diameter, although at closing it is slightly faded in color and remains half-open. On the 4th day the petals fall.

Once the petals drop, the inner receptacle remains. If pollination was successful, the fruit begins to form about two weeks after the petals fall. Then after the fruit and seed pod ripen completely, the pod tilts towards the water. The seeds drop out, leaving the empty seed pod standing.

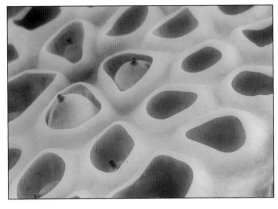

As the daylight length decreases and temperatures drop in the autumn, changes to the plant occur. The last small leaf (stopper leaf) comes out, which signals the thickening of runners into fattened rhizomes to store nourishment that will sustain the plant through winter.

Cultivation

(also see Quick Guide for Gardeners)

Basic Requirements

The lotus has only a few requirements to prosper and reward the owner: a somewhat confined space, plenty of food, sunlight, and enough of a calm water reservoir to prevent it from drying out. Lotus performs well in most parts of the world except those with harsh or extreme climates. It requires at least 5-6 hours of midday sun and at least three months of warm 75–85° F (24–30° C) temperatures. It tolerates brief periods of hot weather but tends to do poorly when summers are very dry or temperatures are consistently 95–115°F (35–46°C), as in the southwestern United States. Cool climates with particularly high rainfall, like the United Kingdom, northern Europe, and southwestern Canada, are not well suited to growing lotus. The overcast skies associated with frequent rain do not allow enough light intensity for the lotus to bloom.

The time to obtain lotus tubers is in the early spring, before they begin growth for the season.

Bare root rhizomes are available for shipping in the spring while they are completely dormant. The tubers should be clean, unbruised, and with growing tips intact. Damp raw sphagnum is the best medium for shipping since it protects the tuber from damage and helps preserve the natural wax-like coating. Whenever handling tubers, use great care since the new growth is very brittle and damage to the growing tips can slow the growth of the plant, or in extreme cases, kill the entire lotus.

Once the temperatures are warm enough for the tubers to begin sending out new growth they are planted and allowed to grow until they become large enough to be presentable for sale. Potted plants can be purchased locally in late spring through summer. After that time the chances of finding lotuses for sale are low.

Soil, Potting, and Depths

Soil should be comprised of good grade topsoil without too much clay or organic matter. Clay tends to compress as the root mass takes up available space. The soil then becomes hard and makes it difficult for the new growth to penetrate. Soil that is too rich with organic matter can spoil or ferment as decomposition occurs underwater and lead to the demise of the dormant tuber. As Patrick Nutt from Longwood Gardens once put it, *"If it grows grass it will grow waterlilies and lotus."* Good soil for lotuses should

have enough clay to stick together when a handful is squeezed but should crumble easily.

Many growers use steer manure in their planting mix but care should be taken that it is well composted and used as an amendment only. Many people report using steer manure with great success but it should be noted that others have experienced difficulty and it caused the demise of their lotus plants.

Lotus has been grown in any number of water holding receptacles from old bathtubs, kiddie pools, and stock tanks to galvanized tubs and the most ornate decorative containers. In the backyard water garden, lotus is usually planted in large plastic containers without holes. The absence of holes is to prevent the plant from escaping and running rampant through the pond. If the container is large enough it can also be buried at ground level in the garden to create a lotus pool.

Lotus will prosper in as little as 4–6" (10–15 cm) of soil in the bottom of the container. The dormant tuber should be placed on top of the soil with the cut end closest to the edge of the pot, which allows plenty of room for the new growth. Press the tuber in enough to keep it from floating up. Top dressing with gravel is generally discouraged because it weights the soil beneath it. A small handful of gravel or a stone can be placed on the tuber to hold it down if necessary.

Active growth circles the bottom of the container as if it is always seeking a way out. It is best if the soil doesn't fill the container completely, so the mass of new growth has room to form, pushing the older growth toward the surface. Each spring decayed growth from the previous year can be removed from the surface without disturbing the tubers that formed the prior year on the bottom thereby reducing the frequency that the plant needs to be divided.

The most successful spring planting strategies maximize the amount of light and heat received by both the tuber and water. Planting from tubers is successful when done in the spring, not later in the season when water temperatures can become too hot. Placing the new plants in shallow water is best since it is important to maintain good light intensity and warm consistent temperatures. The new plants should be protected from extreme temperature changes, both hot and cold. Repotting is also only done in the spring.

Later in the season, lotuses grown in containers are susceptible to pH instability or nutrient imbalance that can cause chlorosis of the leaves. This is usually from very hot conditions and rapid evaporation of water, which leads to high concentrations of calcium in the soil. This will lock up manganese and also raise pH. Keeping the soil cooler (as it is in the bottom of the pond in nature) seems to help prevent the rapid evaporation of water and limit the potential of calcium build up.

As long as the soil doesn't dry out lotus will thrive. Large varieties will grow best submerged to a water depth of 1–2' (30-61 cm) once established. They will tolerate much

deeper depths but it should be noted that deep water reduces the overall height of the plant and may result in only floating leaves. Some people have more success with shallower water depths, since the plant and water heat up sooner in the season. Lotus is also tolerant of bog conditions, as long as the soil remains moist, but the wet conditions of a bog make it difficult to control the weeds that germinate from seed and may compete for space and nutrients.

In large open bodies of water lotus will create lush masses of growth along the shoreline. In order to find new growing areas on the other side of the lake or river, which may be as deep as 25' (8 m) or more, they may send out runners that use the leaves as flotation devices, suspending the roots 8–10' (2.5–3 m) below the surface. This is sometimes referred to as the suspension effect.

Fertilization

The world over it is a well-known fact that lotus is a heavy feeder, requiring a tremendous amount of nutrients to support its stunning growth and flowers. It is important to have a basic understanding of lotus' needs to make a good judgment as it pertains to feeding. For example, experience dictates that newly harvested dormant tubers are not tolerant of high nitrogen fertilizers at the time of planting and that fertilization is best delayed until the plants have several aerial (non-floating) leaves. At that time enough roots have developed to ensure the plant's ability to uptake the added nutrients.

Likewise, before the end of the growing season ample time should be allowed to ensure that nutrients can be consumed for the specific type of fertilizer used.

Remaining unused fertilizer can be detrimental to dormant tubers during the winter months.

Dr. Slearmlarp Wasuwat from Thailand says it is important to note that feeding requirements are specific to the desired outcome. As it applies to N-P-K (nitrogen-phosphorus-potassium), plants being grown for flowers should receive a higher K formula. Root-producing lotuses require a high N-P initially and a reduced N at maturity. Seed lotuses need high N and P.

Examples of popular commercial aquatic fertilizer formulas used for *Nymphaea* and *Nelumbo* are 10–26–10, 10–14–8, 20–14–8, and 12–20–8. In addition to N-P-K, 10 other nutrients are important to promote strong growth and flower formation. They include iron for lush green growth, boron to promote flower formation, and zinc to help regulate plant growth. Select a well-balanced and complete fertilizer whenever possible, including micronutrients.

Commercial aquatic plant fertilizers are available in most parts of the world but are manufactured for a number of different purposes and vary in their chemical composition (urea, ammonium, calcium nitrate, etc.). Raw materials are equally inconsistent depending on the source and/or duration of formulation. For example, manure, compost, and some manufactured fertilizers are high in soluble salts. Salts can pull moisture from the developing foliage and burn tubers or developing root growth. This is why waiting to add fertilizer until after strong growth begins to develop is critical. It is also important to start slowly. Add smaller amounts in the beginning and increase as plant growth increases. Selecting fertilizers specifically

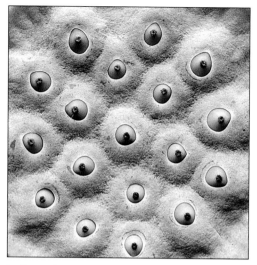

developed for use with aquatic plants will help reduce error.

Fertilizers also vary in their composition and release methods depending on what part of the world one lives in. Some areas do not have access to commercial fertilizers or they are too expensive. So growers may rely on natural resources to provide the necessary nutrients. Dried fish powder, bone meal, ground sheep hooves (similar to bonemeal), dried blood meal, sesame hulls, and soy bean hulls are among the things that are effectively used to feed lotus in less developed countries.

Aquatic plant fertilizers are most commonly available as a slow release tablet so they can be pushed into the soil. (It is important to press the soil back over the tablet after insertion so the nutrients don't release into the water.) The quantity to use depends on the manufacturer's instructions. However, the frequency for lotus usually needs to be increased.

As with all fertilizers, a good way to gauge frequency is to monitor the foliage color. If the leaves begin to get pale three weeks after a feeding, then every 3 weeks will be sufficient. In turn, if the foliage begins to yellow 2–3 days after feeding then the amount applied is too concentrated and the quantity should be reduced. Fertilizers with added humates help increase the availability of the nutrients to the plant.

Basic granular fertilizers like 10–10–10 or 15–15–15 release their nutrients promptly upon contact with the water and small amounts are sometimes wrapped in newspaper to create makeshift tablets to be pushed into the soil. This is an acceptable substitute to tablets but should be applied sparingly and frequently since it is not slow release.

Granular fertilizers also come in slow release or controlled release formulations that release their nutrients based on temperature or moisture exposure. For example, the popular fertilizer, Osmocote®, has a semi-permeable resin coating that releases more nutrients during warmer periods and less during cooler periods. This works in a warmer climate but with much shorter release duration. In the cooler north, water temperatures take quite a while to reach the release temperature and too much nutrient may be released at one time, often too late in the season for the plant to make use of it, with deadly effects. It also may not be ideal in climates with long growing seasons.

Another controlled release fertilizer, Nutricote® (commercial name for Dynamite Plant Food™) releases fertilizer based on available moisture, releasing approximately 25% of the nutrients upon contact with water, with the balance following at a slower pace. It is considered safer than fertilizer that releases via temperature.

It is important to note that this and other time release granular products will not release for the label rated duration when used under water. A formula that is rated at 140 days for terrestrial use will only provide approximately 90 days under water.

Propagation

From Seeds

Viable lotus seeds are very hard, round, and smooth; *N. nucifera* are more oval than *N. lutea*. The infertile seeds will crumble under pressure or have wrinkles like raisins. The hard seed coating is composed of two layers; the outside is dark brown while the inside is light brown. The seed coating needs to be scarified in order for water to penetrate for germination. If only a few seeds are to be germinated a hard file or medium grade sandpaper and a pair of pliers will do. Otherwise a Dremel tool

with a medium sanding bit comes in handy. Hold the seed firmly in the pliers and sand the outer coating enough to expose the lighter brown inner coating. Sanding to the cream color will cause damage to the cotyledon, which can expose the seed to fungal infection. (Note: When using a Dremel tool, the seeds become extremely hot. Take caution not to touch them until they have cooled.)

Once the seed coats have been broken, place the seeds in a glass jar of water in a warm sunny location. If the water becomes

stagnant or cloudy, clean the jar and replace with warm clean water as necessary. In a day or two the normal swelling of the seeds will occur. According to Perry Slocum, the best time to germinate lotus seeds in North America is the first week of May and no later than the 10th. Although his information had no scientific standing, he swore by it. He noted the damping off of seedlings was much lower when germination occurred at that time of year. Generally speaking anytime in early spring is acceptable for seed germination.

When the leaf stems are at least 3" (8 cm) long the seedlings can be transplanted to a more permanent home. It is not necessary to have developed roots when planting and some believe early planting prevents root damage. The seedling should be placed in the center of a 10–12" (25–30 cm) diameter pot of good soil without fertilizer, in shallow water about 6–8" (15–20 cm) deep. The first several leaves will float on the water surface and the plant will begin to form rhizomes. It is important not to add fertilizer until the plants display good vigor and healthy growth. If the plants outgrow the container gently slide them into a larger one so they can gain adequate strength to form tubers for wintering. Flowers shouldn't be expected until the second year.

From Rhizomes

Lotus tubers are collected in the spring. The tubers, which look like bananas connected end to end, are the result of the plants' energy being stored in the fall to wait out the winter. When spring arrives tubers provide the growth for the coming

year and the cycle repeats itself. Some growers have had success growing lotus from midsummer runners. However without the stored energy of the tuber for dormancy, runners are not practical for shipping and there is a significant failure rate, especially if the runners do not have ample time to recover and create tubers for winter.

Rhizomes that are collected from the parent plant often have between one and five segments or more, not all of which will sprout new growth. Some of them will serve as a food source to establish new growth for other segments. The growing tips are pointed and are located at the nodes. At a minimum one to two growing tips are required to establish a plant.

There is considerable disagreement as to whether or not segments with multiple growing tips can be cut apart to increase the number of plants. Although many growers do cut them, there is some evidence that success rates may be reduced due to the increased ease of entry for disease pathogens and fungus. Others believe that the tubers should remain entirely intact for that reason. Additionally there are a number of other reasons bareroot plants may fail to grow: temperature fluctuations, nutrient variables, lack of light, and so on. This is definitely a topic that would benefit from some scientific research.

Tropical lotus are divided by runners and don't require ample time to develop tubers since their growth persists throughout the winter in their favored mild climate. The absence of tuber formation is what prevents them from surviving the harsh winter of a cold climate.

Controlling Unwanted Growth

Occasionally an unsuspecting gardener will plant lotus in an earth bottom pond without the confines of a container. In a fertile pond some varieties will grow 40–60' (12–18 m) per growing season. The rapid growth can quickly overtake a pond. Regain control by cutting the foliage below water level and removing it. This will cause a majority of the plants to drown. Herbicide may then be used to spot treat areas of attempted new growth. Removing the majority of foliage and preventing it from decaying and rotting in the water body will help maintain a higher level of water quality through the control process.

Landscape Uses

Pondscaping

The lotus adds a dramatic element to almost any water feature. Its unique bold leaves are the perfect complement to other foliage types. It provides the perfect vertical backdrop for grasses or flowering marginal plants, acting as an anchor to tie the landscape together, including the waterlilies, other aquatics, and surrounding terrestrial plants.

Because of their height *Nelumbos* make outstanding specimen plantings. Plus the large leaves are so distinctive that the plant looks great even when not in bloom. Consider lotus placement carefully to maximize the sunlight falling on them for both breathtaking views and plant performance. Use of artificial lighting will capture the dynamic foliage after dark. Of course during blooming season their long-lived buds and amazing flowers become focal points and even the unusual seed pods attract attention.

Lotuses are showstoppers so be careful when planning a water garden to ensure they do not block other important design or plant elements. Also remember to consider their deciduous characteristics, unless you have the less common tropical cultivars. Some pond owners like the look of dried leaves and seed pods during winter, others cut them off.

Container Gardening

Nelumbo is equally happy in or out of the water garden. As long as the lotus' basic growing conditions are met, it can pop up amid perennials in the border garden in a buried stock tank or sit above the soil in an upscale or complementary pot. Lotus is suitable to any water-holding container, provided there is adequate depth and diameter for soil and a suitable water reservoir. The containers can be buried so the lotus appears to be growing at ground level, or they can be displayed above ground.

Above ground, any generously sized decorative pot that holds water will suffice. For non-waterproof containers, insert a pot that is waterproof. If the container is too tall and narrow the lotus may be planted in a plastic pot that is supported at a more appropriate depth. Lotuses grown in containers are low maintenance, versatile, charming, and often a stunning focal point on a deck, patio, or entryway.

Four to six inches of soil (10–15 cm) in a 36" (91 cm) diameter x 12" (30 cm) deep container makes a perfect home for *N.* 'Mrs. Perry D. Slocum' buried at ground level in the perennial garden. Large cultivars would be equally at home in 42x15" (107x38 cm) or 58x18" (147x46 cm) containers. Dwarf and medium types should be buried in smaller containers. Remember that all lotuses prefer a wide base to provide plenty of growing room.

Creative Planting Ideas

Lotus displays are only limited by one's imagination. Although a container without holes is the best way to grow lotus, why not push the borders or boundaries? In circumstances where a lotus is given larger areas to roam it will create a very effective and absolutely spectacular display. It could take on a formal, meandering, or free form shape, depending upon the container size or the pond perimeter. Using something besides a standard round container would create larger free form shapes to add interest and reduce the frequency of annual upkeep since the plant can spread freely throughout a larger area. The smaller the growing area the more often it has to be maintained.

When space allows, mass plantings are the way to go. Lotus gardens can be magical and the scent from the blossoms heavenly. A one-acre pond with a quarter-acre or more of lotus snuggled along an edge is an incredible sight. Mass plantings of lotus can also be confined adjacent to the pond by creating concrete barrier walls embedded well into the soil to prevent escaping runners. As long as two bodies of water are separated the lotus will stay within its boundaries. These large stands of

lotus offer impressive foliage and sufficient numbers of blooms to make the fragrance more intoxicating.

Any shape or size adjacent to a water feature is an acceptable space for lotus to grow. It makes an outstanding informal backdrop. The bold foliage and stunning flowers are the perfect complement to statuary and structural features outside the pond. A moat for lotus along the rear side of a water feature lets the plant have free roam, locates it outside the water garden for easier maintenance, and breaks the shape barrier. If properly designed the lotus moat can also act as an effective plant filter. When water is circulated through the lotus growing bed the function is two-fold. The plant gets a steady flush of nutrients to the root system and the

nutrients are removed by the heavy feeding plant—the perfect marriage.

Since few shrubs are actively flowering during the hot summer months lotus should be given strong consideration as a flowering hedgerow. Dig a trough 4' (122 cm) wide by 2' (61 cm) deep by whatever length is suitable. Grade the adjacent property so rain events will keep the trough full of water. The trough can be framed and lined with EPDM rubber liner, topsoil added, and established lotus plants placed approximately every 6' (2 m). The lotus will quickly fill the area and provide a spectacular display throughout the summer months. With that in mind, consider the endless shapes, sizes, and possibilities. (This is the perfect use for scrap liner pieces.) Rigid plastic landscape edging, recycled plastic, or composite lumber can be used to frame virtually any shape from serpentine to arc to semicircle.

A Eocene epoch, India—Fossilized impressions of lotus leaves and rhizomes are dated to more than 34 million years ago, found in a collection bed near Damalgiri. Other fossils of lotus parts have been found around the world, including this one from the United States.

B 3000 BC, Asia & the Middle East—*Nelumbo* is revered as sacred in Hinduism and Buddhism, profoundly significant in mythology, literature, and art. Its many virtues symbolize enlightenment and purity since it grows in the mud but blooms above the water without becoming wet or tainted.

C 1787, Western Europe—Sir Joseph Banks transports lotus from the Middle East to Europe in order to cultivate it for display in the heated tanks of botanical gardens. *Nelumbo's* ongoing and increasing use worldwide in public gardens is a tribute to its universal recognition and popularity.

D 1825, India—A Persian manuscript was found that documents the cultural and economic importance of lotus in everyday life. For example, dried leaves were used to make plates, cups, and other disposable utensils. This practice, plus uses for other lotus parts in food and medicine, continues into modern times.

E 1920s, China—*Nelumbo nucifera* seeds that were collected from a dry lake sediment bed in northeastern China were successfully germinated. In 1990 carbon dating determined those seeds were 1300 years old. In 1952 *N.* 'Ohgahasu' flowered after sprouting from seeds thought to be over 2000 years old, found in Chiba, Japan.

F 1975, Germany—Scientists at the University of Bonn discover the reason for the self-cleansing of lotus leaves. A scanning electron microscope reveals that the leaf's surface is not smooth, but rough at several levels. This Lotus-Effect causes water to form droplets, carrying dirt particles away with them.

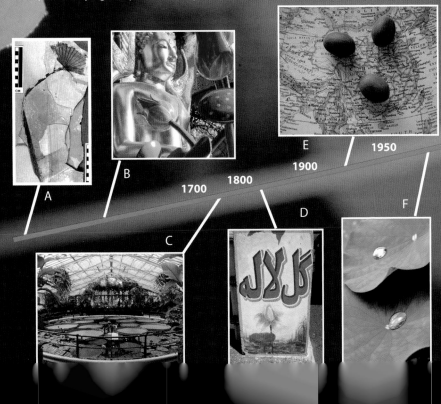

Lotus Timeline

G 1986, India—The Bahá'í House of Worship in New Delhi holds its dedication ceremony. Over 8000 people from 125 countries attend. This modern architectural marvel replicates a half-open lotus blossom and is surrounded by nine round reflecting pools representative of lotus leaves.

H 1990, Japan—Dr. Satomi Watanabe, of Tokyo University, writes the extensive reference book titled *The Fascinating World of Lotus*. The work in Japanese and English details *Nelumbo* species and cultivars as well as the history, cultural significance, morphology, and cultivation of lotuses.

I 1998, Australia—Lotuses intrigue all portions of Oz society from aborigines to scholars at the University of Adelaide. Roger Seymour publishes research confirming the unique ability of *Nelumbo nucifera* flowers to regulate their internal temperature, an extremely unusual quality in plants.

J 2005, United States—For centuries lotus has been used as food and medicine. Now medical imaging allows a view of lotus in an artistic light not previously available. The intricate internal details of the infrastructure are uniquely visible in this amazing x-ray work of art by Jim Wehtje.

2000

K

J

I

H

G

K 2006, Worldwide—Young people of all races and religions folded more than 2,100,000 paper lotuses as part of Singapore's Project Million Lotus. Individuals made the lotuses to show their international support for compassion and harmony. After many centuries, the lotus is still a powerful symbol of purity and peace.

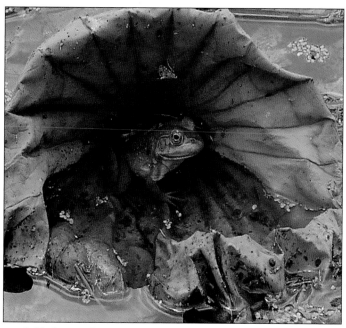

Wildlife and Lotus

Frogs exhibit a natural affinity for lotus, perhaps because of the heat flowers generate or the textured leaf surface that is easy to grab. They can often be found perched somewhere on the plant, bringing joy and surprise to pond owners and photographers. Several wild animals and birds eat parts of the lotus plant or use them for shelter in natural ponds. Fish also find refuge amid its underwater stalks plus countless insects are attracted to the buds and flowers.

Koi have been the root cause of the demise of many waterlilies over the history of ornamental ponds. Their persistent foraging, grazing, and digging in or around the soil of the waterlily roots have made many pond owners

28

throw in the towel. Lotuses on the other hand, are an alternative for koi owners that want lush, dense growth and colorful flowers in the koi pond. Lotus planting containers can be placed in shallow margins around the pond or on constructed pedestals in the center of the pond with the top of the container just beneath the

water's surface so the koi don't have access to the root systems. As an added deterrent, koi don't like the prickly stems of lotus. Lotus is also perfect for separately constructed bog areas, either set adjacent to the koi pond or built within it. The lotus also provides welcome shade for the pond water during the heat of summer.

Similarly, deer predation can be avoided for both lotus and waterlilies if addressed in the planning stages. Both plants are a favorite food of deer. Neither plant can tolerate persistent, heavy grazing of foliage since the tubed stems that are used for transfer of gases let water and sometimes disease to enter. This may render the plants weak to a point that they are unable to survive (a drowning of sorts). If deer are likely to pose a threat, a steep drop to deep water, rather than a sloped or shelved perimeter, will deter them. The absence of easy access or stable footing works to ones favor. Lilies and lotus can then be planted a safe distance from the pond's edge.

101 Other Uses

Food

Seeds

In addition to being eaten raw, pickled, candied, or cooked, the seeds are ground to make flour or roasted to make puffed "makhanas" (like popcorn). It

doesn't take long to become a discerning connoisseur to know exactly which size and color of seed coat will provide the best flavor. The younger seeds are sweet like a cross between sweet corn and young peas. The more mature seeds have begun to get a mahogany cast to the tip and have a much nuttier flavor similar to a chestnut.

Traditionally, peeling the seeds is a necessity since the outermost shell produces a dry feeling in the mouth. Under the first coating is a second milder flavored coating that is usually eaten. Some seed eaters prefer to remove the inner leaf buds prior to consumption. They are sometimes bitter in the more mature seeds, but it certainly isn't necessary. The seed itself has two halves and the leaf buds in the center are worth looking at least once or twice. It is remarkable to see the tiny yet amazingly perfect leaves already formed, ready and waiting.

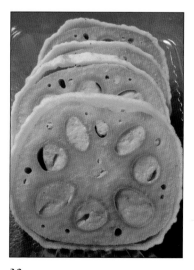

Tubers

Lotus tubers are as important for food in Asia as potatoes are in the United States and are considered a staple. They are used regularly as a vegetable in stir-fry and contain a starchy thickening agent similar to okra or arrowroot. The crisp tubers are also sliced to reveal their beautiful, intricate pattern then baked to make a candy of sorts, pickled in vinegar, boiled in soups, or fried for chips. American Indians also relied heavily on the lotus as a source of food. Depending on the cultivar, location, and cultivation practices, current yields are between 1.6–16 tons per acre annually. Both the seeds and tubers contain calcium, phosphorous, iron, sodium, potassium, plus vitamins B1, B2, and niacin. Only the rhizomes contain vitamin C.

Leaves and Stems

Stems and young leaves are eaten cooked or raw. Mature leaves are heaped with any mixture of meat, rice, lotus seeds, or herbs. The leaves are then folded like a burrito and laid on a grate just above boiling water to steam. The flavor of the leaf penetrates the mixture and after cooking the leaves are unfolded to form disposable

plates for their contents. Paper-thin slices of the leaf stem are soaked in a hot and spicy herb solution and then dried for storage. When ready, the dried slices are fried in hot oil for a zesty, crispy snack.

Flowers and Pods

Almost all parts of the lotus are edible. Even the immature seed pods, flower petals, and stamens are used as garnish or in tea.

Medicine

All parts of the lotus are used for medicinal purposes, either alone or combined with ingredients. Extracts, tonics, astringents, pastes, and individual plant parts have been successfully used to treat cardiac illness, sexual dys-

function, abdominal cramps, bleeding ulcers, hemorrhage, sunstroke, excessive urination, hypertension, insomnia, skin ailments, and ringworm, to name just a few. The whole plant is used as an antidote to mushroom poisoning. Scientific research continues to confirm the effectiveness of the lotus for many

ailments and solidify it as a viable resource for future medicines.

Floral Arrangements

Lotus blossoms as well as the plant have been revered as sacred for over 5000 years and are the most frequently featured flower in Asian artwork throughout history. The flowers themselves are not suitable for flower arrangements since they drop their petals soon after being cut. The buds, however, are used often in floral displays, sometimes numbering in the hundreds for a single arrangement. For stunning displays the buds are used alone or in combination with young green pods, or other complementary cut flowers and foliage.

Often the petals of the flower buds are tucked in or folded to reveal the colorful centers. In the street markets of Thailand and other Asian countries folded lotus flowers are usually for sale. They are commonly used for elaborate arrangements in hotels, business offices, and during religious ceremonies. In the Buddhist and Hindu religions folded lotus flowers are often used as offerings at times of worship since the sacred lotus flower has a number of symbolic meanings including eternity, enlightenment, purity, and good fortune.

Fresh green lotus pods are often combined with flower buds to add interest, texture, and color to the arrangement. Dried pods are sometimes used in silk flower arrangements and may be painted a glittery gold or silver to help them stand out. Imaginative decorators use a multitude of colors for impact. Children also like to let their creative imaginations go wild with vivid colors and patterns on painted pods.

Thread and Fabric

The thread taken from lotus leaf stems is used for making wicks for oil lamps in temples. Stems are also harvested to produce cloth that is primarily used to fabricate monk's robes, ceremonial clothes, and occasionally traditional clothing. Stems collected during the rainy season produce the best threads and must be used within

three days of harvest. The stalks are washed, peeled, and the center threads are collected using a delicate process. The threads are then joined by hand and spun into thin silk-like yarn that is woven into fabric, which is warm in the winter and cool in the summer. Creating the cloth is no small feat and it takes approximately 120,000 stems to produce a set of monk's robes.

Prayer Beads

Lotus seeds are used to create strings of beads called malas, power beads, prayer beads, or rosaries. Other seeds, woods, or precious and semi-precious gemstones are also used for the same purpose. Each possesses its own spiritual meaning. The number of seeds relies on the religion with which it is associated. The beads are intended for counting mantras or prayers as opposed to personal ornamentation or jewelry. No matter what the religion, the seeds themselves are not considered to have power. However they serve to provide a foundation for focusing the inner spirit to connect with its own greater being.

Lotus Blossom Perfume

The fragrance of the lotus is very subtle and defies description. Just like the plant, it seems of both heaven and earth, while also capturing the essence of water. As hard as it is to describe, it is even harder to make concentrated lotus flower oil (absolute). It takes

100,000 *N. nucifera* blossoms to make 1 kilo (35 oz) of absolute, so very little genuine oil has been produced. The flowers, both pink and white, are mainly collected in South India from the wild. The price for a kilo is approximately $4000 US.

Research

The lotus has amazed and baffled people for ages, so it is to be expected that science will try to unlock some of the plant's mysteries. Analyses have been done to discover and quantify all aspects of the *Nelumbo*, from its chemical compounds to its gaseous transmissions to the mathematical relationships of its seed pods to Japanese design. It is no surprise to learn that the lotus is considered one of the most widely researched plants. Here are a few examples of some studies and applications of the findings.

Temperature Regulation

Although many plants are thermogenic, lotus is one of only three that is thermoregulatory, a characteristic normally reserved for animals. Calorimetric and electronic microscopic research confirmed that *N. nucifera* is able to regulate the temperature of its flowers to remain at 86–96°F (30–36°C) when the surrounding air is as low as 50°F (10°C). The flowers both maintain heat and use evaporative cooling. Research continues to determine the exact mechanisms involved as well as to confirm their rationale. The assumption is that its thermoregulation is linked to the increased activity (therefore productiveness) of beetles that fertilize the flowers.

Lotus Effect

The natural cleaning properties of lotus leaves enable *Nelumbo* to grow in muddy areas yet remain spotless. Botanists, chemists, and nanotechnologists have extensively studied this self-cleaning property. They determined that the microscopic structure and surface chemistry keep the leaves from getting wet. They also allow droplets of water to envelop contaminants and roll them off the leaf, leaving behind a clean surface. This trait has been called the lotus effect, a name that has even been registered in some countries.

 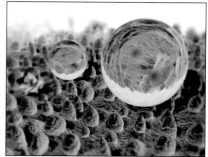

Scientists have been hard at work imitating this effect so the self-cleaning property can be incorporated into products or onto their surfaces. Applications are as wide reaching as roof tiles, house paint, metal surfaces, glass greenhouse panels, and hospital or other garments. Some products are already on the market with others under development. In times past, the lotus effect resulted in *Nelumbo* becoming a symbol for purity. Today it spurs technological breakthroughs and patents.

Crafts and Play

Lotus is an enticing plant for children as well as for adults. The leaves make wonderful hats for either practical use or to allow a child to drift into imaginary worlds. The largest leaves can be used for a perfect umbrella to escape the hot summer sun or rain. Lotus leaves are considered magic by the inquisitive, young and old alike.

Playing with drops of water on the repellent surface has been known to provide hours of entertainment.

In the early fall careful selection of a firm, frost-touched leaf will make an excellent shield for a young warrior. Gnarly, spiked swords may be created from well-chosen sturdy, hardened bloom stems for the ultimate battle.

Others might also enjoy launching their fleet of ships from the pond's edge, as the lotus petals float beautifully on the water's surface. Sometimes small dolls or plastic soldiers floating in their personal petal boats have served as targets in the heat of war. Another use for lotus petals is to gather as many as can be carried to a nearby stream for the *Nelumbo* version of Poohsticks. Opponents release petals at the same time to see whose reach the finish line first. Or they just follow them downstream to see whose can make it the farthest.

Cultural Traditions

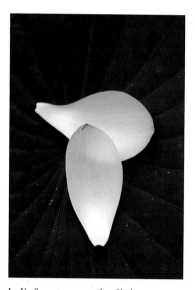

Historically the *Nelumbo* has been at the root of spiritual beliefs in the East and West. The lotus has always held a symbolic importance according to folklore, legend, and early writings, especially in Hinduism and Buddhism. As a result, lotus blossoms embellish ancient relics, statuary, tombs, burial grounds, and temples of worship. This profound foundation has helped shape many ideas about the lotus in modern cultures.

Today *Nelumbo*'s cultural significance remains clearly evident as part of various belief systems and religious ceremonies. The deep rich history of lotus is imprinted and celebrated the world over. This plant is so highly regarded and cherished that it is used in or on virtually any object, from everyday household items to buildings. It continues to provide unwavering inspiration to worshipers and artists around the world.

"The lotus flower holds a special place for us because it symbolizes our struggle in this world. It is born in the still waters of the pond underneath the mud, and, when the time comes, it emerges. It grows out of the water and straight toward the sky, opening its petals in the rays of warm sunlight, revealing its beauty and sharing its fragrance with the world, leaving the mud

far behind. Even its leaves are water resistant, as the flower reaches toward the sky, somehow existing as a part of its environment, and separate from it at the same time."

—The Buu Mon Buddhist Temple
on the significance of the lotus in Buddhism

Lore

References to the lotus appear in literature and art from ancient India to the present. Once you start looking, they show up everywhere . . . Lotus Elan sports car, Lotus Notes software, Lotus the rock band, Light of Truth Universal Shrine (LOTUS), Tesco Lotus the Thai chain store, Lotus Bakeries in Belgium, and the list continues.

Postage stamps with *Nelumbos* have graced letters mailed from countries around the world and the lotus is the national flower of a few countries.

Some *Nelumbos* were given US plant patents in the 1980s.

The Lotus Position is a posture that mirrors that of the lotus blossom. It improves flexibility, encourages proper breathing and invigorates nerves. It is adopted for meditation to seek spiritual insight, tranquility, or the control of mind and body.

During meditation one chant is the mantra, "Om Mani Padme Hum." Each syllable has multiple meanings but it is best summarized as "the Jewel is in the Lotus." This refers to Buddha, who is often shown sitting in a huge lotus blossom.

Lotus Stem Cups are made during the lotus festival in Japan. Wine is poured into the bowl of a leaf with stem attached. A hole is made in the leaf's center so the stem can be used as a straw. This process extracts the life giving juices, as lotus is believed to have been born at the creation of the universe.

In Chinese there are two main names for the lotus flower—He Hua and Lian Hua. Waterlily means sleeping lotus.

The Japanese name for lotus is hasu. This derives from the word for beehive, since its receptacle looks like one.

Nucifera means "having hard fruit."

Statues of Buddha often depict the imprint of lotus blossoms on the soles of his feet. According to legend, at birth he took seven steps in ten directions and a lotus flower appeared each time.

❀

*"I have fallen in
love with you;
Please give me a
drop of honey of
your lotus."*
—Jayadeva

❀

*"The air is filled with the flavors,
and the water is clean;
The moon is lighting dimly;
Every morning I try to listen to the
sound of lotus blooming."*
—Seigen Yanagawa

❀

*"After the shower, the moon dwells
on a lotus leaf."*
—Saigyoh

❀

*"If we could see the miracle of a flower,
clearly, our whole life would change."*
—Buddha

FINE BRUSHWORK PAINTIN
OF GUIZHENG, A SERIES OF LOTUS FLOWE

Quick Guide for Gardeners

Foliage

Leaves are Chlorotic

Deep green veins with yellowing foliage can be caused by both under and over feeding lotus.

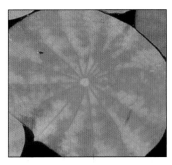

- New plants should not receive commercial fertilizer until several aerial (non-floating) leaves are present. At this time the plants have developed enough of a root system to adequately uptake nutrients. Fertilizer should be halted at least 60 days prior to the expected end of the season to give plants sufficient time to consume all the nutrients before entering dormancy. During the peak growing season fertilizer should be added every three weeks.

Too much fertilizer late in the season will affect overwintering tubers. Rolf Nelson, TX, USA; Do not place fertilizer tablets too close to new developing growth. Cynthia Thomas, CO, USA; Osmocote® caused major salinity problems if the water temperature got too warm and the fertilizer released too quickly. Slow release Landon fertilizer works well but should be added under the soil to prevent burning, rather than mixed in. Tim Schwender, NY, USA

- If using natural fertilizer, steer manure must be well composted otherwise fermentation of the soil can occur. A tablespoon each of dried blood and bone meal can be added to the bottom soil. Dried fish powder can be mixed with water into 1.5" (4 cm) balls and dried to be added later.

Steer manure can be incorporated or layered quite liberally, as lotus seems to need lots of feeding. Elda Rae Yoshimura, HI, USA; We have not had any luck adding manure. We add organic greensand for potash source. Cathy Green, TN, USA

Leaves Turn Prematurely Brown

Leaf burn can occur from pesticides, extreme hot and dry winds, or excess nutrients.

- Lotus foliage is particularly sensitive to some pesticide sprays so all products should be tested prior to a heavy application. Seek products labeled for use on aquatic plants. Damage from extreme weather patterns can be pruned out and new growth will replace it.

Overspray from adjoining properties may unintentionally be the cause of damage.

- When over fertilized, lotus foliage may become brown around the edges. If high nutrient levels are the cause, reduce feeding or replant into less fertile soil. Plants grown outside the pond may benefit from a flush of fresh water to wash away excess nutrients.

We have had problems with browning leaves, which we believe is magnesium deficiency. To prevent this we add about a teaspoon of magnesium sulfate. Rowena and Bob Burns, Ont, CAN

Floating Leaves Only

Lotus begins its life cycle with floating leaves. The failure to generate aerial foliage can be caused by insufficient nutrients or too deep a water level.

• Soil that is devoid of nutrients may not support initial growth. Adding small amounts of fertilizer may provide the necessary nutrients to get the plants up and running. Plants that are started in water too deep waste reserved energy when developing long stem growth and small leaves. Raise plants closer to the surface.

It is important to plant lotus in shallow water where temperatures are warm but not hot. Maintain as consistent a temperature as possible. We are very careful with the timing of the fertilization, since it is critical in a northern climate. We do not start fertilizing until there is an upright leaf. Rowena and Bob Burns, Ont, CAN.

Shredded

Hail damage may completely devastate foliage.

• It is important to follow good pruning practices to prevent water from entering the stems. Withhold fertilizer until foliage has re-established.

Blooms

None

Not enough sunlight. Fertilizer too high in nitrogen.

• Lotus requires at least 5 hours of midday sun to produce blooms. Early morning or late afternoon sun may not have enough intensity for flowering. High nitrogen fertilizers will generate magnificent deep green leaves but it may be at the expense of flower production.

Try switching to another formula such as 10–26–10, 10–14–8, 12–20–8 or similar ratio. A steady supply of nutrients throughout the growing season is also important. Many growers fertilize every 2–3 weeks. We use tablets every 2 weeks till mid-August. Stu Schuck, SC, USA; We use a controlled release with minors, slow and steady, then tablets in April and June. John Loggins, TX, USA.

Blooms Don't Open

In warm climates flowers may not remain open all day. To conserve energy and to maintain a consistent temperature within the flowers they may only be open for a few hours in the very early morning.

• Provide some light shade or relocate to a more protected area.

Do not reduce light levels to less than 5 hours midday sun.

Pests

Aphids

Aphids are often present in the early spring when new soft growth is emerging and sometimes throughout the season when weather conditions are conducive to rampant aphid populations.

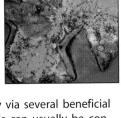

- As shown by the lacewing laying eggs on an aphid populated bud, nature often provides its own remedy via several beneficial insects. In small lotus plantings aphids can usually be controlled by hand early in the season. They often leave the plants once growth has matured. Several products exist on the market that rely on natural substances for effective control of aphids.

Aphids can be a bigger problem when other host plants are nearby.

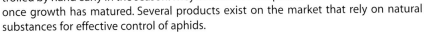

Larvae

Boring and leaf-eating larvae can be present anytime during the growing season. Heavy infestations often begin first on floating leaves. The moth larva chews off leaf pieces then fastens them together to hide inside and float around the pond. Sometimes larvae are attached under leaves or inconspicuously bore a hole in a stem.

- *Bacillus thuringiensis* subspecies *kurstaki* (BtK) is a naturally occurring bacteria that is effective against chewing larvae. The dust can be applied in the evening when the sun is low and should be rinsed off in the morning. Most of the chewing is done at night. Applications may have to be repeated at 7–10 day intervals to get control. As always, follow all pesticide label instructions.

Mosquitoes

Occasionally present prior to active lotus growth. Usually resolves itself as the plant becomes established and the environment becomes more oxygenated.

- If control is necessary, several environmentally safe slow-release mosquito products exist on the market. Follow package instructions. Otherwise a small amount of mineral oil on the surface water will prevent breeding and suffocate any existing larvae.

Predation

Occasionally pruning is involuntarily performed by koi, deer, muskrat, mink, turtles, or other hungry foraging animals.

Establish control measures to keep fish and animals away. Raising the container to a shallow planting area will keep large koi from uprooting plants. Control measures for other animals include trip wires, motion activated water sprays, and relocation of trapped animals.

Planting and Cultivation

Planting Too Deep

Lack of growth or very slow development of newly planted tubers.

- Tubers need high levels of light and warmth to begin each growing season. Start with a good grade of topsoil 4–6" (10–15 cm) deep in a wide, no hole container. Press the tuber into the soil firmly enough that it won't float up, but let it remain on the soil surface.

Do not top dress with gravel, it weights the soil and makes it difficult for new growth to develop. Keep water level shallow to maintain consistent light and temperatures.

Pruning and Deadheading

Selective pruning is often done to remove foliage damaged from insect predation or storms. Deadheading finished blooms, if pods are not desired, will increase flowering. Cutting buds and or green pods can be done for floral arrangements.

- Always cut above the water line to prevent water from entering the stems and inadvertently drowning the plant from the inside out. When water enters the stems it can also carry disease and fungus to the root system. An occasional cut below water isn't usually harmful but repeated or multiple cuts increase the risks.

Winterizing—General

Lotus should be placed below the freeze line to prevent repeated freezing and thawing or extended exposure to extreme cold temperatures.

- Lotuses planted in large containers or en masse survive the winter easier than those in small containers. The old growth and decomposing matter in a large planting generates heat to help protect the lotus during winter. Plants that have been well fed and properly maintained during the growing season have a greater chance of winter survival. Weak plants often fail from disease or fungus rather than the cold.

Fall collected tubers can be placed in a plastic bag, then sunk to the bottom of the pond. In May they can be brought out and planted. Cynthia Thomas, CO, USA; They seem to need a cold period to recharge their battery for spring. Tom Gleeson, AUST

Winterizing—Containers

In cold climates lotus in aboveground containers will be prone to repeated freezing and thawing or excessive freezing temperatures.

- Tip the containers to remove excess water and relocate them to a garage or cold basement for winter storage. They can be placed back outside when extreme cold temperatures are no longer a threat.

We can overwinter lotus in the pots on top of the ground. If it gets below 20ºF (-7ºC) we cover the lotus with frost cloth. Cathy Green, TN, USA

Propagation

Harvest
Rather than being cut apart like other aquatic plants, lotus tubers are collected in the spring.

• Tubers generally congregate in the bottom of the container. Great care should be taken to remove the tubers without damaging or breaking off the growing tips.

For large-scale propagation, other techniques can be used. Before planting, float bareroot tubers in warm water until pink roots appear. Sue See, Ont, CAN

Control of Unwanted Growth
Lotuses occasionally escape their intended boundaries.

• If planted in a container with holes, prune back escaping runners and transplant to a larger no-hole pot. Planting into an earth bottom pond is not recommended unless the intent is for lotus to cover the entire water body. For control or removal from established ponds, cut and remove foliage below the waterline during summer months to allow drowning. Spot treat new emerging foliage with an aquatic approved herbicide until controlled.

Removal of large amounts of growth prior to herbicide application will help maintain water quality and prevent large amounts of decaying matter from reducing oxygen in the water to dangerously low levels. Lotus will not grow out into dry ground.

Resources

Books
These titles either focus on *Nelumbos* or have a chapter about them. They are entirely or have sections in English.

Wang Qichao & Zhang Xingyan. *Lotus Flower Cultivars in China,* 2005. (cont. of 1989 ed.)

Perry D. Slocum. *Waterlilies and Lotuses,* Timber Press, 2005. (1996 ed. with Peter Robinson)

Greg & Sue Speichert. *Encyclopedia of Water Garden Plants,* Timber Press, 2004.

Satomi Watanabe. *The Fascinating World of Lotus,* Parks and Open Space Assn. of Japan, 1990.

Zou Xiuwen, et al. *Flowering Lotus of China,* Jindun Publishing, 1997.

Ni Xueming, ed. *Lotus of China,* Wuhan Botanical Institute, 1987. (on Auburn Lotus Project website)

ONLINE

The Internet is an excellent reference, with thousands of pages with lotus information. The type of information runs the gamut from the psychedelic to the scholarly and from casual observation to scientific research. An excellent way to begin searching is at www.google.com. To reduce the amount of irrelevant information, exclude unwanted terms with Boolean operators (e.g. lotus –car –notes). Instead of "lotus" try "*nelumbo*" to reduce non-essential results. For a more specific search use google features found under *More*. Try *Directory* to group your topics, *Scholar* for academic articles, or *Patents* to index the US Patent Office files.

Visit www.iwgs.org for articles, links to additional lotus info, and specifics about *Nelumbo* registration. Another informational site is www.victoria-adventure.org. Websites of businesses selling *Nelumbo* may have a wealth of photographs and information, as may some botanical gardens and associations.

PLACES TO VISIT

Hundreds of botanical gardens around the world have ponds with aquatic plants. The number of those with exceptional lotus displays is far fewer. Below is a very small sample of international gardens, parks, and temples* that feature *Nelumbos*. They may have lotuses in natural lakes, landscaped ponds, water gardens, or museums. Some are not on typical lists and might be a bit harder to find. Inquire at your local botanical garden or temple for noteworthy lotus gardens in your region. Remember that the best time for lotus viewing is during the heat of summer, generally between early July and late August in the Northern Hemisphere.

UNITED STATES AND CANADA
Auburn University Lotus Project, Cullman, AL www.ag.auburn.edu/hort/landscape
Ganna Walska Lotusland, Santa Barbara, CA www.lotusland.org
Modesto Lotus Garden, Modesto, CA www.lotusgardens.com
*__Meishoin Jodo Temple,__ Big Island, Hilo City, HI
*__Hooganji Shingon Temple,__ Big Island, Hilo City, HI
*__Buu Mon Buddhist Temple,__ Port Arthur, TX www.buumon.org
Kenilworth Aquatic Gardens, Washington, DC www.nps.gov/kepa
Keith McLean's Lotus Ponds, Rt. 1, Morpeth, Ont, Canada

EUROPE
Vivai Bambu Credera-Rubbiano, Italy www.vivaibambu.com

CHINA
Bai Yang Dian, Hebei province
Beijing Botanical Garden, Beijing www.beijingbg.com/en_index.htm
Hangzhou Hua Pu, Hangzhou. site for 19th Lotus Conference
Lotus World, San Shui, Guandong province.
Lian Hua Chi, Beijing
Waterlily World, Qingdao, Shandong province. site for 18th Lotus Conference
Wuhan Botanical Garden, Wuhan, Hubei www.whiob.ac.cn/english

JAPAN
Atagawa Tropical & Alligator Garden, Kamogun, Shizuoka Prefecture
Hanahasu Kouen, Minami Echizen, Fukui Prefecture
*__Jodo-shu Daihonzan,__ Kamakura, Kanagawa Prefecture
Kodairen no Sato, Saitama Prefecture
Kusatsu Aquatic Botanical Garden, Mizunomori, Kusatsu, Shiga Prefecture
Kyoto Flower Center, Kyoto Prefecture
*__Mimurotoji,__ Uji, Kyoto Prefecture

EVENTS

Each year lotuses enter the spotlight at many botanial gardens and municipalities around the world. They become the star of festivals, holidays, and conferences. Check with your local botanical garden, chamber of commerce, or temple for scheduled festivals, garden and pond tours, holidays, or Asian celebrations that might feature lotus. Events are usually scheduled during the best lotus viewing times. July and August are when most lotus events are planned in the United States and Asia, including the International Lotus Conference in China and the 2007 IWGS Symposium in Thailand.

PHOTOGRAPHY AND ART CREDITS

Photographers and artists retain copyright © to the listed images. Used with permission.

T = Top, C = Center, B = Bottom, L = Left, R = Right

Auburn University Lotus Project: 14B
Luce Beaulieu: 26-B
Paula Biles: 2, 15, 17T, 19B, 23T, 26-E, 26-F, 27-H, 31B, 38T, 38BR, 39CT, 41T, 41B, 48T, 50, 51
Kelly Billing: 22C, 23C, 23B, 24T, 24C, 32C, 35BR, 39T, 42T, 43–4 images
Susanne Bund: 10T, 17B
Andy Davis: 39CB, 45
Benoit J. Schecter Demacon: 18, 36
Denver Museum of Nature & Science, Image Archives: 26-A
Jeremy Feig: 27-G
Keith Folsom: 13B, 14T, 19T, 20, 38BL
Laura Grant: 6B
imagedj.com: 11B, 37TL
Greg Jaehnig: 37BR
RBG Kew: 26-C
Kanchana Kokhakanin: 31T, 31C, 32T, 33B
Grant Mitchell: 4, 7–13 images, 8T, 8B, 9T, 10B, 11T–4 images, 16, 21, 26-D, 27-I, 28B, 29B, 30T, 35TL, 35TR, 35CL, 35BL, 37BL, 39B, 40T, 40C, 40BR
Larry Nau: 37TR
Nees Institute for Biodiversity of Plants (Univ. of Bonn): 34L
Michael Oberman: 12B, 37CL, 46, 47
Pete Orelup: 33T, 49
Shinichiro Saka: 12T, 25, 37CR
Dick Schuck: 22T, 40BL
Paul Shiah: 51B
Perry D. Slocum: 6T, 24B
Surfnux and CxNi: 27-K
Takashi Tomooka: 32B
Garet Uemura: 9B, 30B
Janet Wasek: 13T, 28T, 29T, 42B, 48B
Jim Wehtje alternativephotos.com: 27-J
Wikipedia.com: 34R

Front cover—*Nelumbo* 'Pekinensis Rubra' Rev. Lao X. Do © 2007
Back cover—Susanne Bund © 2006

ACKNOWLEDGEMENTS

Special thanks go to Grant Mitchell for his steady stream of inspiration, amazing photographs, endless new hybrids, and his wonderful addiction to lotus. Thank you to Stephen Blessing, Bob and Rowena Burns, Keith and Tish Folsom, Tom Gleeson, Cathy Green, Randy Heffner, John Loggins, Christopher and Suzanne McMahon, Rolf and Anita Nelson, Patrick Nutt, Jim Purcell, Stuart Schuck, Tim Schwender, Sue See, Cynthia Thomas, Garet Uemura, Primlarp and Dr. Slearmlarp Wasuwat, and Elda Rae Yoshimura. They provided regional details based on their own experiences with *Nelumbo*, which helped shape several sections of the book. Many others helped with the creation and writing of this book, like Rosie Smith who did an outstanding job of layout. We hope that we didn't omit anyone. Kelly gives a special thank you to Colleen, whose amazing creativity, wisdom, and thirst for knowledge always serves as an inspiration. And to Matthew, who is growing up loving lotus and nature the way she does. Paula offers appreciation to all her students, who motivate and spur her to keep learning more. Last but not least, each of us would like to express our deep appreciation and thanks to the other half of this writing team; it has been a remarkable and truly complementary effort.